SEA OTTERS

Glenn VanBlaricom

Colin Baxter Photography, Grantown-on-Spey, Scotland

SEA OTTERS

First published in Great Britain in 2001 by
Colin Baxter Photography Ltd
Grantown-on-Spey
PH26 3NA
Scotland

www.worldlifelibrary.co.uk

Text © Glenn VanBlaricom 2001

WorldLife Library Series

A CIP Catalogue record for this book is available from the British Library.

ISBN 1-84107-085-8

Photography Copyright 2001 by

Front Cover © Tom and Pat Leeson
Back Cover © Mark Newman (Bruce Coleman Inc.)
Page 1 © Kip F. Evans
Page 3 © Art Wolfe (Art Wolfe Incorporated)
Page 4 © Art Wolfe (Art Wolfe Incorporated)
Page 6 © Henry H. Holdsworth
Page 9 © Len Rue Jr. (Leonard Rue Enterprises)
Page 10 © Len Rue Jr. (Leonard Rue Enterprises)
Page 12 © Michael H. Francis
Page 13 © Renee DeMartin
Page 15 © Kennan Ward (Kennan Ward Photography)
Page 16 © François Gohier (Ardea London)
Page 18 © Jeff Foott (Bruce Coleman Inc.)
Page 19 © Tom & Pat Leeson
Page 20 © Colin Baxter
Page 23 © Image State
Page 24 © Johnny Johnson (Bruce Coleman Collection)
Page 25 © Ken Lucas (Ardea London)
Page 27 © François Gohier (Ardea London)
Page 28 (Top left) © G Ellis (Minden Pictures, FLPA)
Page 28 (Top right) © Ken Lucas (Ardea London)
Page 28 (Bott. left) © Ken Lucas (Ardea London)
Page 28 (Bott. right) © Stuart Westmorland (Tony Stone Images)
Page 30 © François Gohier (Ardea London)

Page 31 © Leonard Lee Rue III (Leonard Rue Enterprises)
Page 32 © Doc White (Ardea London)
Page 35 © Michael H. Francis
Page 36 © François Gohier (Ardea London)
Page 39 © Kip F. Evans
Page 40 © Jeff Foott (Bruce Coleman Collection)
Page 41 © Johnny Johnson (Bruce Coleman Collection)
Page 43 © David B. Fleetham (Oxford Scientific Films)
Page 44 © Norbert Wu (NHPA)
Page 47 © François Gohier (Ardea London)
Page 48 © Henry H. Holdsworth
Page 50 © Frans Lanting (Minden Pictures)
Page 51 © Art Wolfe (Art Wolfe Incorporated)
Page 52 © Henry H. Holdworth
Page 53 © Doc White (Seapics.com)
Page 55 © Henry H. Holdsworth
Page 56 © François Gohier (Ardea London)
Page 58 © John E. Swedberg (Ardea London)
Page 59 © John E. Swedberg (Ardea London)
Page 60 © Renee DeMartin
Page 63 © François Gohier (Ardea London)
Page 64 © Henry H. Holdsworth
Page 67 © Art Wolfe (Art Wolfe Incorporated)
Page 68 © Henry H. Holdsworth

Printed in China

Contents

Introduction   7

Otters at Sea   11

Connections to Coastal Marine Environments and Ecosystems   17

Life Raft   37

Population and Conservation Biology   49

Public Involvement in Sea Otter Conservation   69

Distribution Map   70

Facts and Recommended Reading   71

Index   72

Introduction

It is a rare night in Prince William Sound, Alaska. Neither rain nor snow is falling and the wind is at rest. It is winter 1978, and very cold. The black sky is riddled with the silver-blue of distant stars. Low on the northern horizon the faint green *aurora borealis* dances in silence. I am in a narrow bunk in our research cabin, located on the quiet shore of Gibbon Anchorage at Green Island. Two colleagues are in repose across the small room, one snoring thunderously. My sleep is interrupted and my mind is puzzling, but not over the deafening uproar so close by. It is a different sound, much softer and more distant, which has my attention. It comes in cycles, repeating perhaps every minute or two. First the gentlest of splashing sounds; then in rapid succession come three 'crunching' sounds; then a pause of a few seconds; then more crunches and another pause, and yet again several times over. Finally comes another gentle, brief splash and the quiet returns. The entire sequence lasts for perhaps 20 or 30 seconds. Another minute passes in silence and then it begins again.

Foraging in the quiet darkness of the cove, a sea otter dives to the bottom perhaps 16 feet (five meters) below. Her descent causing a brief swirl of water at the surface, she quickly probes the muddy substratum for a favored prey – bent-nosed clams – living just beneath the sediment surface. She finds the clams in clusters, each one perhaps 1 to 1½ inches (3 to 4 centimeters) in length. Methodically, she pulls them one at a time from the mud, stowing them in the loose axillary folds of skin where her forelimbs join her shoulders. The mud billows from the bottom in dense clouds as she works, but it is her deft touch, not her eyes, which leads her to her chosen prey. After a minute she ascends swiftly, splashing gently as she reaches the surface. She draws breath and settles on her back, comfortably afloat. She quickly draws a clam from her axilla, pops it into her mouth, chews it shell and all, and swallows it down. Another clam is drawn out to suffer the same quick fate. And

An adult male sea otter grooms quietly prior to a rest period in Kachemak Bay, Alaska.

another, and another. Crunch! Crunch! Crunch! Pause. Crunch! Crunch! Crunch! With no clams remaining she lifts her head, quickly scans the circle of her surroundings and descends again, leaving the characteristic swish of water in her wake.

There is a short list of mammals whose inexplicable appeal overwhelms our best efforts to be logical and dispassionate. Koalas, pandas, gorillas and killer whales elicit joy, admiration and empathy from human observers. Brown bears, porpoises, wolves, orangutans and chimpanzees interest us in part because they pose challenging dilemmas in conservation policy, but mostly because we are irresistibly drawn to them for reasons entirely beyond science. Sea otters are surely on the list as well, but the story barely begins with their charismatic appeal. Interest in sea otters encompasses several other compelling concepts. Firstly, sea otters are among the most ecologically important of animal species living in the coastal seas of the North Pacific Rim. In many locations, marine ecosystems are very different with sea otters present than without. Secondly, few species in the sea are more vulnerable to the damaging effects of spilled oil than sea otters, and few commodities are more desired by modern human cultures than petroleum products. High demand means high rates of transport of crude oil and refined products by tank ship, and increased risks of accidental spills of catastrophic scale in sea otter habitats. Thirdly, sea otters are the vexing, tireless enemies of people whose lives are devoted to the harvest of shellfish at sea for sale on shore. Equally happy with clams, crabs, abalones, sea urchins and even octopus as items of food, sea otters are formidable competitors for shellfish resources.

For the past 24 years, sea otters have provided me with a wellspring of scientific questions. The labels for sea otters are endless, some reflecting appreciation and awe, others anger and frustration. I invite you to learn about these remarkable animals and share my good fortune in trying to understand their ecology and their interactions with humankind. In all likelihood you will come up with your own label along the way.

Adult sea otters rest, as they form a small 'raft' near a kelp forest on the California coast.

Otters at Sea

There are 13 modern species of otter, and populations are found on all continents except for Australia and Antarctica. Several species utilize coastal marine habitats, in some cases feeding in the sea but breeding and socializing primarily on land or in lakes and rivers. Two species are considered to be marine mammals. The marine otter (*Lutra felina*) lives in the coastal zone of southern Peru, Chile and southern Argentina. The smallest of all marine mammals, marine otters breed and rest on rocky shores and feed primarily on small crustaceans taken from nearshore marine waters. The sea otter (*Enhydra lutris*), smaller than all marine mammals other than the marine otter, is the only otter capable of living its entire life free of contact with land. All major life functions of sea otters can be done at sea including: feeding, breeding, birthing, socializing and resting. Some sea otters utilize land by choice, primarily for resting and occasionally for giving birth. Sea otter populations in northern portions of the species' range are more likely to be found resting on land, probably because 'hauling out' on shore provides some benefits in retention of body heat, especially in winter months. In general, however, sea otters are truly marine mammals.

All modern otters have elongate flexible bodies, with four short limbs modified to varying degrees for swimming. Otters have thick fur composed of two hair types – guard hairs and denser, shorter underfur. The latter traps air against the skin when the animal is immersed, thus serving an important function in heat conservation. Broad muzzles support long whiskers that are important sensory devices for locating and seizing prey. In some species, the forepaws also have unusual tactile sensitivity and serve important functions in detection and capture of prey. Otters compose the subfamily lutrinae of the mammalian family Mustelidae, a large group of carnivores, which includes stoats, weasels, martens,

An adult female sea otter checks her surroundings prior to a foraging dive.

badgers, skunks, wolverines, ferrets and minks, among others.

Life at sea imposes important constraints on the lifestyle of sea otters, as it does for all marine mammals. The result is an important suite of adaptations, which clearly set sea otters apart from other otter species. The hind limbs of sea otters have been fully modified into flippers, somewhat like those of the harbor

Sea otters spend long periods grooming their fur everyday.

seal. In all other otter species the rear limbs retain clearly defined paws, although interdigital webbing is an obvious adaptation to aquatic life in most cases. Sea otters are strong swimmers and excellent divers compared to other otters, and the flipper-like rear limbs are the primary source of propulsive thrust. On land, sea otters are far less agile and mobile than other otter species. Front limbs of sea otters are more like other otters, but the digits are fully enclosed in simple paws that are like mittens. Seemingly cumbersome by design, the front paws are remarkably sensitive to the shape, size and texture of objects encountered, and enable a grip that is surprisingly sure.

The fur or pelage of sea otters is modeled on the general pattern for other otters, but the density of individual hairs per unit of skin area is higher than that of any other mammal on earth. Retention of an insulative air blanket is more important for sea otters than for other otters, and the extreme density of hairs

Older sea otters often have strikingly white or light gray fur on their heads and upper bodies.

– up to 150,000 hairs per square centimeter – is an important evolutionary result. In contrast, most people have fewer than 100,000 hairs on their entire heads and many of the experienced marine biologists that I know have far fewer than that!

Because sea otters spend more time immersed in water than other otter species, heat loss is a problem even with properly functioning fur and an intact air blanket against the skin. As a result, sea otters must replace lost heat by increasing the rate of metabolism. Metabolic rates are higher for sea otters than for other species of similar size, as a consequence of heat loss associated with constant immersion at sea, and the relative imperfections of the fur as a thermal barrier.

Most otters have sharply pointed teeth in the back of their jaws to allow shearing of the flesh of their most common prey – fish. This pattern is seen in many other mammalian carnivores as well, such as lions and foxes, which feed primarily on the soft tissues of their prey. Sea otter teeth are very different, with flattened molars that crush rather than tear. Many of their prey species, such as clams or mussels, have hard shells and must be crushed in order to be eaten.

Before large-scale harvesting by people began in 1741, sea otters were found from the northern shore of the island of Hokkaido, Japan and eastward around the North Pacific Rim to the outer coast of peninsular Baja California, Mexico. Sea otters typically are associated with fully exposed outer-coast habitats, but they may have been common as well in semi-enclosed marine habitats such as Prince William Sound, Alaska and San Francisco Bay, California. Many people are surprised to learn that sea otters are habitat generalists and are not limited to rocky coastlines. They do very well in some bays and estuaries where the sea floor is primarily mud or silt, and they are also able to live along exposed sandy beaches in some places.

Dependent sea otter pups rest on their mothers' chests as their fur is scrupulously groomed.

Connections to Coastal Marine Environments
and Ecosystems

Water in the ocean takes up heat from a submerged warm object about 25 times faster than air at the same temperature. Marine mammals have internal body temperatures very similar to humans – about 99°F (37°C). All marine mammals must be able to tolerate full immersion in sea water for months at a time, and in some species for their entire lives. Survival depends on an effective thermal barrier that minimizes heat loss, and a metabolic system capable of immediately replacing lost heat. Most marine mammals, including whales, dolphins, porpoises, seals, sea lions, walruses, manatees and dugongs, solve the problem with a layer of fat, normally termed 'blubber', deposited immediately beneath the skin. Blubber is a fundamental adaptation that allows marine mammals to survive in all the world's seas, including frigid polar waters in both hemispheres.

Like other otter species, but unlike most marine mammals, sea otters lack a significant blubber layer below the skin. The air blanket system is their primary thermal barrier. Although the pelage of sea otters is incomprehensibly dense, it does not work as well as blubber in limiting heat loss, primarily because the air blanket is relatively thin. The only remaining option is for sea otters to make heat internally as fast as it is lost. High rates of metabolism can be sustained only with high rates of food intake. Consuming prey at an extraordinary rate – in order to maintain body temperature at the desired physiological equilibrium – sea otters influence their biological surroundings at a level far disproportionate to the numbers of sea otters or their individual body masses. Food consumption rates by sea otters have been estimated at 25-38 per cent of body mass per day. Imagine a person weighing 176 pounds (80 kilograms), routinely eating 44 pounds (20 kilograms) of food per day!

Sea otters have distinctive grooming patterns crucially important to the

Squid are vulnerable to sea otter predation when in shallow water.

maintenance of the fur as a thermal barrier. They may spend up to 20 per cent of their time each day in grooming activity. Grooming includes intensive rubbing of all parts of the pelage, which is often is augmented by simultaneous somersaulting and blowing of bubbles in the water, facilitating the addition of new air to the air blanket against the skin. Grooming time is a favorite among regular visitors to captive otter displays in zoos and aquaria, and never fails to entertain. If grooming is not done scrupulously, the coat quickly becomes fouled and matted, the air blanket is lost and the fur ceases to function as a thermal barrier. In most cases death is not far behind.

Sharp sea urchin spines are no deterrent to foraging sea otters.

In their search for nutritional and metabolic sustenance, sea otters are able to exploit many species of prey. Most are relatively large invertebrates living on the sea floor in water less than 328 feet (100 meters) in depth. Therefore, most of their foraging is done close to shore. Over 100 species have been identified as sea otter prey. Among them are tiny limpets no larger than a thumbnail, and enormous species such as the king crabs of the Gulf of Alaska, or the giant octopus of the northeastern Pacific.

Along rocky shores, sea otters generally feed on sea urchins, abalones, snails, crabs and octopuses. In some locations they will forage in the rocky intertidal zone, making shallow dives to surf-swept rocks to gather mussels, snails, urchins and crabs. On rare occasions sea otters will leave the water to obtain prey, but such behavior has been seen only a few times. Along stretches of sandy habitat, exposed to large ocean waves, sea otters feed primarily on crabs and clams. As in rocky habitats, sea

Sea otters consume crabs systematically, piece by piece.
Claws are dispatched first, then the legs one by one, and finally the body.

California's Big Sur coastline remains remarkably unspoiled, and provides vital habitat for sea otters.

otters are quite comfortable in the surf zones of exposed sandy beaches, foraging successfully directly beneath crashing breakers. Only the very largest waves seem to diminish their willingness to look for food in physically dynamic locations. As previously described, sea otters are effective clam predators in the mud and silt bottoms of semi-enclosed marine habitats. Sea otters will locate prey visually when daylight is sufficient and the water relatively clear. They also capture prey easily at night and in murky waters, in such cases depending on touch by their forepaws to find prey items on the sea bottom.

In some places, sea otters are known to forage on certain bottom-dwelling fishes. Such patterns seem to occur primarily in the northwestern portion of their range, especially in the western Aleutian Islands, Alaska and the Commander Islands, Russia. There are also a few unusual cases of sea otters taking seabirds as prey. Such cases seem to involve single individual otters and may be limited to older males.

On average, foraging sea otters dive for about a minute at a time, usually in depths of 100 feet (30 meters) or less. The deepest known dive by a sea otter is 328 feet (100 meters), the greatest duration about five minutes. Dive patterns vary by habitat and may be influenced by the depth distribution of preferred prey. Sea otters are the strongest divers among the 13 modern otter species, but are weak divers compared to other marine mammals.

Sea otters tend to alternate feeding episodes of several hours with rest periods of similar duration. Although there are always exceptions, the foraging patterns of sea otters tend to be synchronized. Off California's Big Sur coastline, sea otters typically begin foraging early in the morning, then enter a rest period from mid-morning to mid-afternoon. They forage again from late afternoon until dusk. For obvious reasons nocturnal patterns are not as well documented, but available data from animals with telemetric instruments suggest a third foraging period near midnight. It is not known if prey species taken at night differ from those taken during the day.

Prey species such as snails, mussels, sea urchins, or crabs are quickly and routinely wrenched from substrata by the overwhelming strength of the otter's paws and forelimbs. Likewise, on the surface such species are normally dispatched quickly by powerful jaw muscles and teeth adapted for crushing as noted above. Small mussels are chewed and swallowed whole, including the shells. Larger ones are held briefly between the paws, the paired shells separated with an abrupt twist, exposing the soft tissues. Sea urchins are bitten through from the underside where spines are shortest, the contents then licked out with the tongue. Crab shells are quickly removed by deftly inserted canine teeth, after which the animal is devoured, wholly and quickly.

Clams and abalones require special capture techniques and all large prey individuals, regardless of species, may require specialized handling techniques on the surface before they can be consumed. Clams typically must be dug from sediments on the sea floor. Digging of clams by sea otters has been directly observed by scientists only rarely – it is largely a matter of chance. In over 2000 hours of research scuba diving during my career, I have had only one opportunity and most of the event was obscured by the clouds of silt raised by the digging otter. Digging behavior is much like that of the family dog burying a bone, with rapidly alternating front-to-rear strokes of the forelimbs, excavating a pit of increasing size as the otter works downward into the sediment. When pits become large and clams are abundant, the otter may work on the sides of the pit rather than the bottom, laterally expanding it and allowing exposed clams to fall from pit walls toward the center. Otters generally prefer large prey items, and larger clams tend to live deeper in sediments. However, it appears that the great energy required to dig very large pits involves a point of diminishing return. Thus, clams living deeper than 20 to 24 inches (50 to 60 centimeters) in the sediment may be less vulnerable to predation.

Capture of abalones requires the use of tools, a rare skill among mammals. Abalones are primitive snails with a very large 'foot' and an enormously strong attachment to rock surfaces. Human divers cannot possibly dislodge abalones without specialized pry bars. Sea otters have a more direct approach. The tool of choice is a smooth flat rock, often 6 to 8 inches (15 to 20 centimeters) in diameter.

An adult female rests with her pup on a patch of kelp in the littoral zone of Alaska. The more northerly sea otter populations prefer to rest onshore, while more southerly populations tend to rest in the water.

A young sea otter concludes a feeding period. Sea otters often spend 6 to 8 hours foraging a day.

Once the unfortunate abalone is located, the foraging sea otter sets to work pounding the abalone shell with all the strength it can muster. Abalones partly hidden in rock crevices remain vulnerable as long as the otter can chip away at a shell edge. Only those deeply withdrawn in narrow crevices have a chance to escape. The otter continues to bash away until the shell breaks or the animal capitulates and loses its hold of the rock. Often more than one dive is required to complete the job. In California years ago, my colleagues and I watched sea otters make 20 or 30 consecutive dives, each time surfacing with the tool rock tightly clutched under a forelimb, each time diving again in the exact same spot, until finally, triumphant and perhaps with the smallest hint of swagger, the otter brought up an abalone.

Black turban snails near Moss Beach, California.

The same flat tool rock can be used skillfully as an anvil in order to process prey for consumption. Once on the surface with prey in 'hand', the tool-bearing sea otter assumes the normal posture, floating on its back with head tilted forward. The tool rock is balanced over the center of the sternum or breastbone. Prey items are held between the forepaws and in short, mechanically advantageous arcs swung sharply against the rock in repetitive rapid succession. The process continues until the shell fails and the soft tissues can be extracted and swallowed. Certain small prey species also require use of an anvil before consumption. For example, turban snails are abundant in California's coastal environments and are common sea otter prey. The snails are rather small, reaching perhaps 1 inch (3 centimeters) in maximum diameter, but their shells are robust and highly reinforced. Sea otters cannot crush the shells and ingest the turban snails without first whacking them a few times against an anvil.

An interesting variation on tool use is seen when sea otters are feeding on hard-shelled clams in sandy habitats where stones are not available. Here, sea otters often bring two prey items to the surface. One is balanced on the sternum and serves as the anvil, while the other is processed and consumed. This approach works well as long as the otter can find at least two prey items at a time. One day I stood with a colleague on the public pier at the town of Pismo Beach, watching sea otters feed on Pismo clams. Pismo clams are a heavy-shelled species of shallow water along exposed sandy beaches. The otters had been working the area around the pier extensively and the number of clams available had diminished. We saw a young male otter with one clam securely tucked into an axilla. He dove repeatedly, but could not find a second clam. Periodically he would stop to rest, bring the clam to his mouth, bite at the unforgiving shell and, in frustration, even pound the clam against his chest. Again and again he would dive, and again and again he would resolutely probe the equally stubborn clam in hopes of breaking through. Finally, just as the sun dropped into the western sea, the otter gave in. Resting quietly on the surface with his gaze averted, he released his grip and allowed the clam to slide from his chest. In the growing darkness he moved off to the north after an embarrassed glance in our direction.

Sea otters seem to have different individual foraging patterns, both for the type of prey they prefer and the methods used for prey capture and handling. The variation among individuals is apparent, even if comparison is restricted to animals of the same age and sex foraging in the same kind of habitat. One individual may feed primarily on turban snails, another mainly on small crabs and yet another on sea urchins. The individual tendencies are consistent through time. The preference of a particular individual is learned from its mother. If an adult female prefers to eat small kelp crabs, all of her offspring are likely to have a similar preference for kelp

An adult male sea otter dismembers a rock crab.

The red sea urchin is a favorite food item.

Box crabs – an invertebrate species eaten by sea otters.

Clams are dug up from the substratum and devoured.

crabs. The tendencies of a mother are probably passed to her offspring by simple imitation. Sea otter pups approaching independence often forage side by side with their mothers; the process of learning by imitation appears to be quite strong, extending to preference for food type. There is also evidence that other aspects of foraging behavior, such as the type of tool rock preferred, are passed down from mothers to offspring.

Some aspects of sea otter foraging are consistent among individuals. Consumption of rock crabs is a good example. Once an otter places a crab on its chest, the moveable 'fingers' on the claws of the crabs are quickly bitten off. Rock crabs are large animals with powerful claws, capable of delivering a nasty and painful injury to the unwary. Experienced sea otters are well aware of the potential, but the learning process may be unpleasant. One day in California I watched an obviously inexperienced young male try to subdue a large crab. Male sea otters have certain private parts well exposed while they are floating on their backs. This particular animal had not yet learned the consequences of failing to disable the claws of the crab immediately. The crab briefly escaped the otter's paws, scuttled across his abdomen, and obtained a firm grip. The otter sat bolt upright in the water and screamed in outright terror. I suspect that he learned his lesson, or lost his taste for crab!

Sea otters are known to have a number of important effects on their prey populations and ecosystems. Scientists have had many opportunities to watch changes in prey populations and ecosystems as sea otters have recovered from near extinction a century ago. It is possible to gather data on numbers and sizes of prey animals, and on other ecosystem attributes, such as plant density and species diversity, in sea otter habitats before the otters return. As the otters return and increase in number, continued data collection on sea otter foraging activity, prey size and abundance and ecosystem features, provides valuable information on the consequences of sea otter presence.

For highly preferred prey species such as sea urchins, abalones, large crabs and large clams not deeply buried in sediments, the appearance of sea otters in areas where they were previously absent has a predictable effect on prey populations. Numbers of prey are reduced, and larger individuals are removed from prey populations. In rocky habitats a third pattern is seen, especially for abalones and sea urchins. The arrival of sea otters is often accompanied by a sharp increase in the proportion of prey found only in 'cryptic microhabitats' such as deep cracks or crevices in the rocks. One of the results of this effect is that abundance of abalones and sea urchins is often directly related to the number of cracks or crevices present

A stranded abalone is finished off by scavenging crabs and snails.

in the rocky substratum. Off the Monterey Peninsula in California, the deeply incised granitic rock supports many abalones even though sea otters are abundant. Just 62 miles (100 kilometers) to the north, the smooth sandstone bottoms off Santa Cruz County provide few suitable refugia; consequently, abalones are quite rare. The abalones off Monterey are relatively small. As they grow to a size too large to remain in the narrow crevices, they have no choice but to move out into open habitats. In the presence of sea otters they do not survive for long.

Modifications of prey populations by sea otters produce a number of interesting and sometimes controversial indirect effects on the structure of coastal ecosystems. The best-known cases involve sea urchins. Sea urchins along the coast of the North Pacific Rim are herbivores, feeding primarily on kelps and other algae that grow on rocky surfaces near shore. When sea otters are absent, sea urchin populations will grow very large if other predators are absent and reproductive

Comfortably at rest in a kelp 'wrap' off California, this sea otter views the photographer with thinly veiled disdain.

*Kelp forests in the North Pacific Rim are productive habitats with many
species of invertebrates as residents. Sea otters often prefer to use kelp forests both for
foraging areas and for resting sites. Here, a harbor seal cruises among the kelp fronds.*

rates are high. Plant populations may be overgrazed, with the result that the ecosystem takes on a barren appearance with few organisms present other than the abundant urchins and a few thin algal crusts on the rocks.

Sea otters are among the most significant predators of sea urchins in the North Pacific, and in their absence urchins may be quite common, particularly off Alaska. As sea otters recovered from excessive fur harvests of previous centuries, ecologists noticed many places where barren habitats were changing into productive and diverse kelp forest communities. These ecologically dramatic shifts were reported from the Aleutian Islands of Alaska, the Commander Islands of Russia and the Big Sur coast of California. However, as reports were published in scientific literature controversy developed, particularly among scientists working in California. Several were quick to point to a number of places in California where diverse and productive kelp forests existed without sea otters. Studies ultimately revealed that in California habitats, a number of factors can limit effects of sea urchin grazing, even when sea otters are absent. More recently it has been discovered that effects of sea otters on kelp forest communities are more extensive along outer-coast habitats, fully exposed to the pounding of ocean waves, than in semi-enclosed marine bays and estuaries. Today marine biologists generally have accepted a consensus synthetic view that sea otters can be important to kelp forest communities, particularly in the northern part of their distribution. However, they also acknowledge that other factors, independent of sea otter foraging, can also influence urchin grazing in the same way and produce the same effects on biological diversity and productivity.

Important ecosystem-level effects of sea otters are not limited to kelp forest communities. In the rocky intertidal habitats of western North America, mussels are a dominant species for attachment space on the rocks. Left undisturbed, mussels are able to overgrow other species and crowd them out. At the same time, mussel beds are complex three-dimensional structures that provide vital habitat for many other species. Thus, predators or disturbances that reduce mussel beds will also reduce groups of species using mussel beds for habitat. However, they also enhance opportunities for species that compete with mussels for space on rocky surfaces. When sea otters feed on mussels, they often create gaps in mussel cover, tipping the balance in favor of other species that require space on the rocks for attachment. Likewise in sedimentary habitats, sea otters create local disturbances when digging for clams. Some species are affected negatively by the disturbances, while others are able to exploit the disturbances as an opportunity. For example, small mobile predators such as sea stars or flatworms may obtain feeding opportunities when sea otters turn over the sediment and expose prey species otherwise hidden.

Sea otters have a preference for many of the same prey species sought by shellfish fisheries. This problem was first recognized in California in the 1950s. Abalone fishers, working south of the Big Sur region, began to notice sea otters foraging on large abalones in preferred fishing grounds. Not long after, harvest rates began to drop drastically. Most scientists were skeptical that sea otters could destroy a shellfish fishery. Complaining fishers were met with the rebuttal that over-fishing, not sea otters, was the real problem. Debate about the issue became confusing and convoluted because there are in fact a number of cases of damaging over-utilization of shellfish stocks. Abalone fisheries are known to be particularly difficult to sustain. However, after years of sometimes bitter, politically charged debate, there is a grudging consensus that sea otters and abalone fisheries cannot co-exist.

Over the last several decades similar stories have emerged for other kinds of shellfish fisheries in other locations. Commercial, recreational, or subsistence fisheries for Dungeness crabs, red sea urchins and various clam species have been eliminated for all practical purposes by the foraging practices of recovering sea otter populations. It is interesting to note that large populations of shellfish species probably did not occur before sea otters were reduced in numbers and distribution by the fur trade. Thus, the harvestable stocks of shellfish, damaged by recovering sea otter populations existed only because sea otters had previously been depleted.

Small kelp crabs are important to the nutrition of sea otters.

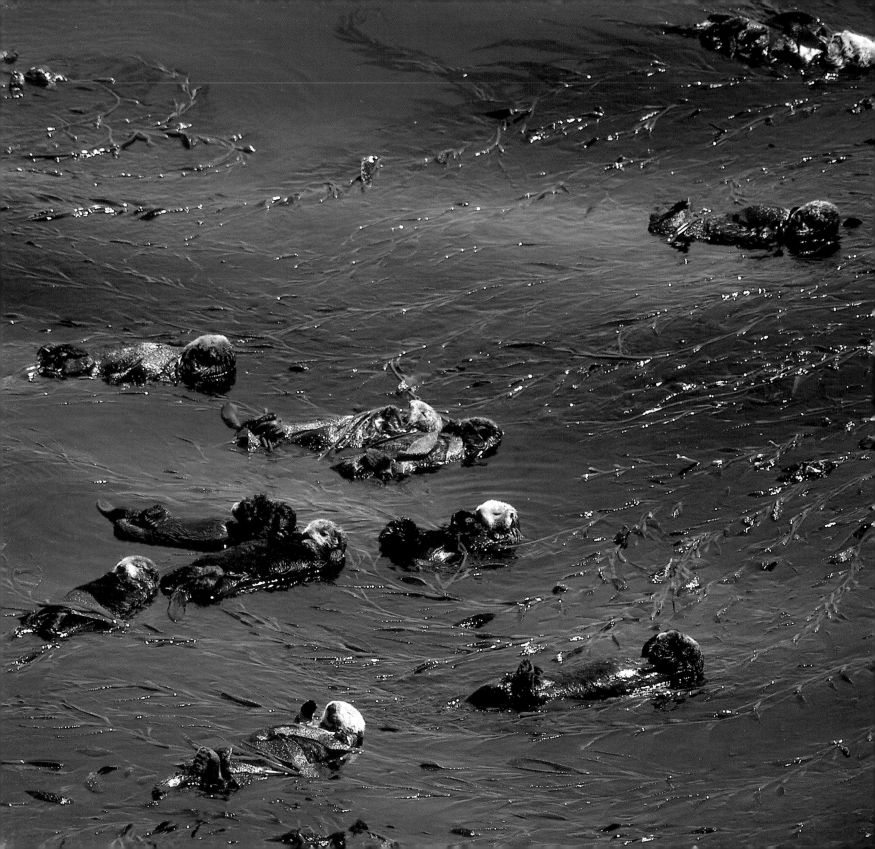

Life Raft

Many aspects of the life history of sea otters are not well-known. The explanation lies in a problem common to most studies of marine mammal ecology. Seemingly simple questions such as life span, age of first reproduction or interval between births are difficult to answer for animals in nature, unless individuals can be identified and followed through time. Marine mammals are particularly difficult in this regard. They live for many years, move around a lot, are difficult to track, spend a great deal of time under the sea surface, out of sight, and are hard to separate from one another. There are a few exceptional cases, mostly involving whale species, where individually characteristic natural markings allow biologists to track individuals and obtain valuable life history data. For most marine mammal species, including sea otters, natural markings are not adequate to allow reliable identification of individuals. In these cases tagging of animals is the only option for collecting good life history data.

Two approaches have been used to tag sea otters. One is the attachment of colored plastic tags to the webbing between the digits of the hind flippers. One tag is placed in each flipper. By varying the color and position of the tags on the flipper, it is possible to produce a large number of individually distinctive combinations. The tags that work best are swine ear tags, which are appropriately sized, very sturdy and durable, and are made in a number of different bright colors. The tags have numbers, but observers rarely can get close enough to read them even with a good spotting telescope. Color and position normally provide the needed information about individual identity.

The second approach is to attach or implant an electronic telemetric device on an animal. The most common type of device is a radio transmitter that broadcasts a simple pulsing signal on a unique frequency across a range of a few

Rafted sea otters at rest in a kelp canopy off California.

miles. The transmitters are equipped with batteries that last one to three years and are encased in biologically inert plastic. The standard model weighs about 3½ ounces (100 grams) and fits easily in the palm of one's hand. These devices are often used to study the biology of seals, sea lions, or fur seals, and are attached to the coarse fur on the backs of the animals. A smaller model weighs about half an ounce (15 grams), has a battery life of a few months, and is roughly the size of one's thumb.

Sea otters have very loose skin and the most flexible bodies of any marine mammal species. As a result, there is no part of the body surface that a sea otter cannot reach with its mouth or forepaws. Consequently, attachment of tags to sea otters is a difficult problem. Most experiments with external attachment failed because the otters simply ripped the tags away from the body regardless of attachment method. Flipper tags are the major exception, providing a relatively secure method. A hole is punched in the interdigital webbing and part of the tag is squeezed through the webbing. Even so, some otters chew and tug on the tags until they are removed. The small transmitters described above can be attached to flipper tags. Some are demolished in a matter of minutes after tagging, crushed between the otter's irrepressible molars. Others survive, the otters apparently untroubled by their presence. There is no way of knowing in advance which individual otters will tolerate flipper tags and the attached transmitters. The larger, longer-lived transmitter packages are impossible to attach to sea otters externally. This has led to the development of a controversial, but largely successful, method for surgical implantation of the package into the abdominal cavity of sea otters. Once attached or implanted, otters can be tracked with a combination of visual observation and telemetric monitoring using frequency-scanning receivers and directional antennas.

A second important technique for studying life histories of sea otters is use of internal growth layers in the teeth. The number of growth layers discernable in sectioned teeth correlates with the age of the individual animal. Teeth can of

A resting otter adjusts position at sunset off California. Once the paws have dried during rest periods, otters will undergo great contortions to avoid rewetting them until the rest period is over.

course be obtained from dead animals found on beaches, or by extraction from live animals under sedation. The first premolar of sea otters is small and vestigial, and can be removed easily without affecting the foraging ability of a live otter. Techniques for sectioning, staining, and reading layers in teeth are now reasonably well developed, producing reliable age estimates for individuals.

All forms of tagging and tooth extraction from live animals require captures in the field. Three methods are commonly used. One involves modified fishing nets. This method is non-selective, but can sometimes allow capture of large numbers of animals in a relatively short time. A second method involves a simple, hand-held dip net and a fast-moving boat. This method allows effective capture of juvenile sea otters, one at a time. The dip net method does not work on the more wary and wily adults. The third method involves a trap operated by divers working with electric scooters and sophisticated rebreather units that release no bubbles. Sleeping otters can be approached from below and captured efficiently. This method is costly and labor intensive, but has the advantage of allowing capture of previously selected animals of any age or size.

All resting periods begin with a good yawn.

Sea otters live for about 10 to 15 years, with females living slightly longer than males. At full size, adult males are usually 66 to 77 pounds (30 to 35 kilograms) in mass, females 44 to 55 lb (20 to 25 kilograms). Captive animals in zoos and aquaria may live quite a bit longer than wild animals. Etika, for years a favorite of visitors to the Seattle Aquarium, died at the age of 28 years, which is thought to be the current record for longevity. Several other captive animals have survived past 20 years of age. One possible explanation for the apparent difference in longevity between captive and wild animals is the influence of tooth wear. Sea otter teeth become worn and ineffective in older animals. Also, wild animals with worn teeth probably experience difficulty in processing typical hard-shelled prey items, resulting in inadequate nutrition and increased mortality. Captive animals with worn teeth may benefit from access to provided food from which hard shells have been removed. Nutritional quality remains high, resulting in greater longevity. Wild animals are subject to many other risks from which captive animals are protected.

Mussels are common sea otter prey.

Female sea otters may mature physically as early as their second year, but most do not become reproductively active until they are four years of age. Male sea otters mature physically when five or six years of age, but do not participate actively in reproduction until a few years later. Most males can mate only if they can maintain breeding territories, and territorial success often relates to body mass and experience. Good territories are in places preferred by females of breeding age. Females probably use two primary criteria in selecting habitats. Firstly, food must be readily available. A breeding-age female will have high metabolic needs during pregnancy and during lactation following the birth of her pups. Food availability is also important in allowing dependent pups to learn to forage, and to improve the chances that weaned pups will survive. Secondly, habitat must include features that provide shelter from heavy weather and seas. Survival of pups is poor if they become separated from their mothers during storms. In California, large kelp canopies provide needed shelter and are highly preferred by breeding females. In Prince William Sound, where kelp canopies are less common, preferred habitats are those close to good feeding grounds. Bays or coves, such as Gibbon Anchorage, also provide reliable shelter in bad weather.

The central goal of a territorial male sea otter is to exclude other males from locations selected by breeding females. If successful, the male will have the opportunity to mate, free of competition from other males, with the females that choose to live in his territory. Female distribution apparently is not influenced by the territorial male, therefore, females can move among territories if they so desire. Males patrol territorial boundaries, usually associated with landmarks or the margins of kelp canopies, to exclude other males and to evaluate the reproductive receptivity of females.

Males excluded from territories tend to congregate in separate groups. Male areas are typically found in more physically exposed locations avoided by breeding females. Male groups sometimes include tens to hundreds of individuals living in close proximity, and typically involve the most intensive social interactions seen in sea otters. As in other mammal species with sexual segregation, play behavior is rampant in male sea otter groups. Extensive chasing, wrestling, biting and vocalizing are all common – often with multiple participants. Play behavior in male groups may establish dominance hierarchies among the animals as they reach territorial status, but verification is lacking.

Within the breeding portion of sea otter habitats, the ratio of females to males is about five to one, with some variation among regions. Because territorial males have the highest probabilities of breeding with the females in their territories, it is thought that each male mates with several females during a breeding season. Males are usually larger than females; the heads and necks of male sea otters typically are broader and heavier than those of females.

A dependent sea otter pup shares a kelp 'wrap' with its mother during a rest period.

Sea otters rest in a 'raft' off the California coast. Gulls often follow otters in hopes of stealing a bit of food. However, these otters are not feeding, and the gulls are wasting their time.

Breeding territories are normally maintained by male sea otters from spring through to autumn. This pattern varies to some degree among locations. Females give birth most often in spring months. Like other marine mammals, but unlike other otters, litter size in sea otters is almost always one. In rare cases of multiple births, only one pup survives. Pups remain with their mothers for about six months, weaning in the fall. The time of weaning is also the time of a brief estrous period in females. Thus, most mating occurs in the fall. Once the period of estrous passes for females, the males often will relinquish defense of territory until the following spring. Typically, large males will defend the same territory year after year.

The most familiar images of sea otters are the 'rafts' of females – with dependent pups and the occasional territorial male – that form in breeding habitats when the animals rest. Although sea otters tend to be well spaced and rather independent when foraging, they become social at rest. Resting groups range in size from a few animals up to 15 or 20 in California, and may be larger farther to the north. When rafted, most animals either rest quietly or groom. Resting animals often are side by side with others. Animals that have just completed a period of foraging typically groom energetically when they first join the raft, rolling and blowing bubbles while furiously rubbing their fur with forepaws. As they settle in, the intensity of grooming declines until the animals appear to be washing their faces or rubbing their eyes. Finally, they become motionless and settle into a wary sleep.

Sea otter habitats are often windy places. Because sea otters have strong affinities to specific locations, they will try to avoid displacement by the wind. The most common solution is to use kelp plants, which are attached to the bottom and rise to the sea surface. Kelp fronds are leaf-like structures covered with a thin but slippery layer of mucous. Holding onto such material while asleep is not easy. Sea otters solve the problem by taking hold of the end of a kelp frond, and then rolling themselves up in the kelp, much like one would roll paper around a cardboard tube. The result is a resting otter, its middle wrapped in several layers of kelp and its head and rear protruding. On very windy days the jostling effect of the waves force the otters to 'rewrap' every 15 minutes or so. Rewrapping can be comical to observe. Comfortably at rest with limbs dry and warm, otters exhibit extraordinary contortions in order to rewrap without rewetting the limbs.

Newborn sea otter pups weigh about 4½ pounds (2 kilograms). The newborn pups have a dense natal fur that confers the look of a ball of fluff. The natal fur is much longer and less well organized structurally than the fur of the adult. The natal fur helps limit heat loss to the air on cold or windy days, but probably does not improve heat retention in water. Pups spend a great deal of time perched on their mothers' chests, nursing from one of two nipples located on the lower abdomen. However, mothers must still forage while caring for the pup. While pups are very young they are simply dumped into the water to wait, floating about on the surface, while their mother searches for prey below. Newborn pups float like corks, swim only weakly and cannot dive. They squeal and cry frequently, especially while the mother forages. The frequent cries, easily detected by human observers on shore and striking in their similarity to the English word 'me!', probably help the mother to relocate her pup following a foraging dive. Sea otter pups begin trying to swim and dive at about one month of age. Initially they are hopelessly inept, in part because of the extreme buoyancy associated with the natal fur. At three months of age the natal fur is largely shed and is replaced by an adult type of pelage. Now the pup swims and dives with increasing confidence and eats solid food provided by the mother after foraging dives. Foraging skills come more slowly, and the learning process probably continues well beyond the age of weaning. Survival of the first winter of independence is determined largely by the young otter's mastery of foraging lessons given by the mother.

During rest periods the sea otter may awaken briefly and groom quietly.

Population and Conservation Biology

In 1741 a Danish mariner, Captain Vitus Bering, sailed from the Kamchatka port city of Petropavlovsk-Kamchatskiy to explore lands and resources to the east in Alaska. With the crew of adventurers was a brilliant, but cantankerous, German naturalist G.W. Steller. Two vessels were involved in the expedition, the *Saint Peter* and the *Saint Paul*. Early in the expedition the vessels became separated, the crews lost confidence in their captains and shipmates and the bickering and recrimination spun out of control. Steller, anticipating the scientific opportunity of a lifetime, fell into such disfavor during the eastward part of the voyage that he was afforded only a few hours of frantic exploration on Alaskan soil during only a single landfall.

On the return journey matters grew worse, culminating in the wreck of the *Saint Peter* on the island that now carries Bering's name, about 186 miles (300 kilometers) east of Kamchatka, and dooming the crew to a winter in the wilderness. Captain Bering perished during the ordeal, along with about 30 crew members. Steller, a pariah at the time of the wreck, became a hero. He applied his scientific training to find antiscorbutic plants for the scurvy-wracked crew and tended to the ailing with skill and care. Although in poor health himself, living in desperate squalor through violent storms and drifting snows, Steller was able to record the first scientific field observations ever made of the sea otter. He also made notes about another species unique to the Russian Islands, an aberrant, giant relative of the manatee later to be known as Steller's sea cow.

I stood at the grave of Captain Bering during the summer of 1992, with Russian and American friends and colleagues. The site is a gently rolling grassy slope on Bering Island, overlooking the reef that doomed the *Saint Peter* and the shoreline where the shipwrecked explorers huddled and suffered during the winter of 1741-42. It is the birthplace of the scientific study of sea otters, the Holy Grail for the sea

In Kachemak Bay, Alaska, a drowsy sea otter sneaks a quick 'safety peek' with one eye.

otter biologist. Nearby, carved on simple wooden planks, weathered by decades of unmerciful gales, are the names of those who perished. Faintly, but unmistakably, I heard their voices in the wind.

In spring of 1742, the surviving members of the Bering Expedition were able to assemble a crude wooden vessel from the salvaged remains of the *Saint Peter*. The final 186 miles (300 kilometers) back to Kamchatka were navigated in a harrowing journey of desperation, and the survivors were saved. Steller died before he could

At low tide, a female sea otter grooms her pup.

return to his native Europe, but his precious field notes were preserved. The ensuing period of fur harvest, stimulated largely by the observations of Steller, became one of the most significant periods of economic and cultural transformation in the history of the North Pacific region. Dominated first by the Russians, but later joined by the Americans, the British, the Spanish and others, the hunt for sea otters was on. There were probably about 200,000 sea otters in the North Pacific at the time of the Bering Expedition in 1741. By the beginning of the twentieth century the harvest had reduced total sea otter numbers to about 2000. They were scattered, a few dozen here and a few dozen there, among 13 remnant groups. In 1911, the Treaty for the Preservation and Protection of Fur Seals was signed by Japan, Russia, Great Britain and the United States. The Treaty included an article imposing a moratorium on the continued harvest of sea otters. This international agreement was clearly the defining act that saved sea otters from biological extinction. Unfortunately the Treaty

In late afternoon at Kachemak Bay, Alaska, a sea otter ends
a foraging period and contemplates a nap.

was too late for Steller's sea cow. Numbering only a few thousand individuals and confined to Bering Island and nearby Medney Island in Russian waters, the enormous, docile sea cows were ideal targets for sea otter hunters in need of food to sustain their hunt for fur. Only 27 years after Steller's notes were recorded, the sea cow was extinct. Steller's notes survive as the only observations of living sea cows made by a trained scientist.

The indigenous human cultures of the North Pacific did not fare much better than the sea cow at the hands of the sea otter hunters. These diverse, proud, culturally rich communities were systematically deceived, abused, enslaved, or murdered by otter hunters of all nationalities. The cultural genocide extended from the Aleutian Islands to Mexico. Many of the First Nation cultures of the North Pacific were lost forever. Those that managed to survive suffered institutionalized abuse through most of the twentieth

This orphan is being rehabilitated as part of a rescue program.

century, long after the sea otter hunters were gone. Despite continued racism and repression, these peoples are beginning to see progress in their efforts to recover the fragments of their past.

For sea otters the twentieth century was a period of recovery, restoration and recognition. The saving of the sea otter is indeed one of the great success stories in marine conservation. Several of the small populations surviving in 1911 subsequently went extinct, either because of poaching, or simply because local numbers had dropped below the critical threshold necessary for the survival of a population. Fortunately, most of the remnant populations began to grow, at last free of hunting mortality. In 1997, at an international workshop in the small town of Forks, Washington, U.S.A., scientists from Japan, Russia, Canada and the United States estimated that about 125,000 sea otters lived in the North Pacific at the time, an increase of about fiftyfold over numbers present in 1911. At the workshop, the perception was that sea otters were fully recovered in southwestern Alaska and the Aleutian Islands, and nearly so in the sea otter habitats of Russian waters. Large populations were reported from southeastern Alaska, smaller but growing populations in the coastal habitats of British Columbia and Washington. The well-known California population was thought to be growing, and there were encouraging reports about recent recolonizations of sea otter habitats in Japan and Mexico.

During the 1960s and early 1970s, translocations were used in attempts to re-establish sea otters off southeastern Alaska, British Columbia, Washington and Oregon. All but the Oregon project were successful. In the case of Washington and Oregon, dispersal and mortality of animals at release caused initial numbers to drop to low levels. In the Washington case, the population survived the 'bottleneck' period, and now numbers over 600 animals growing at about 10 per cent per year. In the Oregon case the population did not survive the bottleneck period for reasons not understood. The most recent translocation project involved movement of animals from the California population to San Nicolas Island, off southern California. About 150 animals were moved between 1987 and 1991. To the great surprise of involved biologists, including myself, many left the island soon after release despite excellent habitat quality, making the remarkable journey of several hundred miles back to the locations of their capture. Dispersal from the island indicated that we had underestimated the affinity of sea otters for a familiar home range. At present, the island population is about 25 animals. Thus, the colony is still in the bottleneck period and survival is uncertain.

In the twenty-first century, we now face the task of making certain that hard-won progress in sea otter recovery is not lost. In the 1970s, concern emerged that

increased development of offshore oil resources posed threats to the sea otter population of California. It was known that sea otter fur lost its thermoregulatory effectiveness if soiled and matted; consequently, there was fear that spilled oil would contaminate many animals, dooming them to quick death by hypothermia. There were reports of sea otter mortalities associated with a spill of fuel oil in Soviet coastal waters in the 1960s, but little detail was available. Documented reports of oil spill effects on sea otters were otherwise lacking, although various laboratory studies, small-scale field experiments and assessments of coastal winds and currents off California were consistent with the notion of a significant threat. Because of its small size and limited range, the California population was officially designated as 'threatened', as defined by the U.S. Endangered Species Act, in 1977. Nevertheless, oil industry representatives, some U.S. government agencies, and many scientists remained skeptical about the risk posed by oil spills to sea otters.

In 1980 I monitored reports of a disabled tank ship named the *Prince William Sound*. Fully loaded with oil, its single engine stopped by mechanical failure, the tanker drifted without power or control in strong southeasterly winds. It traveled slowly across Prince William Sound for a distance of about 37 miles (60 kilometers), past a frightening succession of rocky islets, pinnacles and reefs. Finally, as winds pushed the vessel toward the iceberg-strewn waters of Glacier Island, a line was secured to a tug and a disastrous grounding was averted. At the time, I mentioned to a few colleagues my view that a great oil spill disaster in sea otter habitat would occur somewhere soon, most likely in Prince William Sound. They shrugged and the comments were forgotten. Other observers had similar experiences. You didn't have to be a fortune-teller or a rocket scientist to see what was coming.

Nine years later the helmsman of a fully loaded oil tank ship known as the *Exxon Valdez* turned his ponderous vessel out of the shipping channel, concerned about small icebergs ahead. He never regained his course. Instead, for reasons that remain a mystery, he drove his vessel hard onto a well-marked rocky reef and into infamy. Some 260,000 barrels of crude oil spilled into Prince William Sound. For 24 tension filled hours, the spilled oil rested in a pool in Valdez Arm, only a short distance from the stranded tank ship, while politicians, administrators and oil company executives debated the response options. Before they could act the weather and the sea settled the issue, a passing weather front stirring the Sound and spreading oil for hundreds of miles. To this day I still recoil physically at the memory of the simple radio message from a patrol vessel of the United States Coast Guard, 'Green Island is going under'.

There is no longer any doubt about the significance of oil spills for sea otters. Ironically, scientists cannot agree on the number of sea otters lost to the *Exxon Valdez* disaster. The problem is that the spill was not anticipated, except by a few biologists to whom no one in power would listen. Thus, high quality pre-spill counts of sea otters in the Sound were not available. Nearly 1000 oiled carcasses were recovered, and estimates of mortality range up to several thousand. Response to the spill by managers and scientists was chaotic, primarily because the necessary contingency plans had not been thought through, and the process had not been taken seriously. Likewise, there were no functioning facilities available that could accommodate the rush of oiled sea otters and seabirds soon to be gathered up by rescuers.

Nearly 400 sea otters were rescued alive from the spill area and brought to hastily assembled treatment centers. Many died as veterinarians struggled to identify injuries and develop treatments. As anticipated, many of the mortalities were caused by hypothermia as oiled otters frantically, but fruitlessly, groomed matted fur to restore thermoregulatory function. Other gruesome, unexpected injuries were also detected. Many of the sea otters had severely damaged livers. In their panic to restore their contaminated fur, the otters swallowed some of the oil. Their livers were destroyed as the highly toxic oil overwhelmed their internal chemical defenses. Others had bizarre gas bubbles in their bodies. Sea otters surfacing in or near the spilled oil inhaled the thick, toxic fumes, corrosive to delicate biological tissues. Lungs developed lesions and gasses leaked into body spaces, sealing the fate of the otters.

Twelve years after the disaster, sea otter populations in Prince William Sound

*High-pressure water spray was used to remove spilled oil from shorelines
after the Exxon Valdez disaster. Many scientists argue that the spraying projects
did more harm than good to nearshore biological communities.*

have yet to recover from the oil spill. The failure to recover is most obvious in areas that were most heavily oiled. A number of costly studies have been done to understand the slow recovery. The prevailing view is that lingering effects of residual spilled oil are important, possibly causing long-term problems for sea otters and serving to limit population growth. Chronic oil effects may be interacting with low food supply, the latter caused by natural factors apparently not related to the oil spill. The combination limits population growth in affected areas. Statements that Prince William Sound is fully recovered and once again pristine are not consistent with data from the post-spill studies of sea otters.

At the time of the Forks workshop in 1997, there was optimism that recovery of sea otter populations would continue. Since then new concerns have appeared and the optimism has been dashed. The paramount issue is a precipitous decline in sea otter numbers in the very heart of the sea otter range, the Aleutian Islands of Alaska. Available information indicates that food supply for sea otters remains adequate and the condition of surviving sea otters is healthy. Thus starvation and disease do not seem to be the problem. The favored hypothesis is that sea otters are experiencing increased predation by killer whale populations. The whales, normally feeding on fish, seals, sea lions and porpoises may have shifted their diet because of large-scale changes in the marine ecosystems of the North Pacific. Some scientists argue that these changes have resulted from human activities, especially over-fishing. Others argue that the changes are beyond the control of human actions and are a consequence of natural fluctuations in food web dynamics of the North Pacific. There is much work to be done before the issue is resolved and time is short. The workshop group convened again in November 2000 in Monterey, California. Participants were stunned by the data from Aleutian habitats indicating declines of 70 per cent or more in sea otter populations over the past decade.

The California sea otter population also is a center for new concerns. Sea otters in California survived as a remnant population, probably with fewer than 100 individuals, in the Big Sur region in 1911. From then until the 1970s, the California sea otter population steadily expanded its range, with numbers increasing at a rate of about five per cent per year. During the 1970s and 1980s changing fishing practices caused increased rates of accidental catching of sea otters in fishing nets. Population growth rate seemed to decline, but new fishing regulations apparently solved the problem. By the mid-1990s, discussions centered on the possibility that the population might soon be removed from the list of threatened species. Since then it has become clear that the population is not growing and may in fact be in decline. Possible causes include higher-than-realized rates of drowning in fishing nets, effects of contaminants and effects of newly emergent diseases and exotic parasites. As in the Aleutian Islands, causes for the new problem have not been clearly established, and substantial research work will be required before problems can be pinpointed and management responses developed.

In the first few years following the fall of the Soviet Union in 1991, Russian sea otter biologists reported an alarming increase in poaching of sea otters along the coast of the Russian Far East. The increase in poaching apparently resulted from economic desperation. In the chaos that followed the dissolution of the U.S.S.R, communities in remote locations were largely left out of emergency economic plans, and had few options for survival. A black market for sea otter pelts was ready and waiting in southern Asia, and legal penalties for sea otter poaching in Russia were trivially small. Increased poaching was the inevitable result. Fortunately, the problem has not escalated into a crisis.

With encouragement from the Otter Specialist Group of the Species Survival Commission, World Conservation Union, the Russian government increased penalties for sea otter poaching and expanded enforcement efforts. Economic circumstances in the Russian Far East remain difficult, but poaching of sea otters seems to have declined as an alternative for increased personal income. Only in portions of the Commander Islands does poaching persist as a matter of concern. At present, the Russian sea otter populations appear to be among the most stable and secure of all populations in the North Pacific Rim, containing between 15,000 and 20,000 individuals.

Sea otters are effective sea urchin predators, and in some cases the removal of grazing urchins may allow the size of kelp forestst to increase. Here, a kelp harvesting vessel cuts kelp from the surface of a large bed in California. The kelp harvesting industry is worth over $50M per year. Harvested kelp is used to produce algin and pharmaceutical products.

On warm sunny days, otters will hold their rear flippers underwater while at rest to avoid overheating. On this cool day off Alaska, the flippers are held high, dry and crossed to conserve heat.

In the 1960s and 1970s, communities of indigenous peoples in the United States began aggressive defenses of their interests within state and federal court systems. Tribal representatives argued that explicit rights to fishery and wildlife resources, guaranteed to the tribes in Treaties signed with the U.S. federal government during the 1850s, were being illegally and systematically denied by the actions of regional governments and resource management agencies. Many tribes in the western U.S. had signed Treaties, often under direct military pressure, relinquishing claims to many traditional lands and agreeing to live on reservations. In return, the U.S. government guaranteed traditional fishing and hunting rights to the tribes. In a series of remarkable decisions, courts ruled that government repression of tribal fishing and hunting rights had indeed been illegal, and that the various provisions of the Treaties remained fully valid. Since that time native communities have been able to re-establish harvests of a number of fish and wildlife resources, reasserting a measure of community identity and dignity that had been repressed since the time of the Bering Expedition. Ironically, the passage of the U.S. Marine Mammal Protection Act of 1972 also asserted tribal hunting rights for marine mammals in Alaska.

At present, coastal communities of indigenous peoples in Alaska and Washington conduct legal hunts for a number of marine mammals in U.S. waters, including whales, seals, sea lions, walruses and sea otters. In the past decade, Alaskan natives have taken an average of about 500 sea otters per year, primarily from Prince William Sound and southeastern Alaska. Although these harvests are legal and often involve cooperative regulation among tribal governments and state and federal agencies, they remain highly controversial to the interested public. The renewal of whaling off the Washington coast by the Makah Nation in 1999 further elevated the public controversy, pitting hard-line preservationists against defenders of the restoration of tribal cultures. There is no way to know future actions of tribal communities, but there is reason to expect that expanded exploitation of sea otters may occur. Many coastal tribes, not currently involved in sea otter harvest, have hunted sea otters in previous centuries. Such activities may be welcomed by shellfish fishery interests who see sea otters as competitors for resources. However, tribal harvests will almost certainly be condemned by conservationists who point to the long, difficult recovery of sea otter populations, the known significance of sea otters to ecosystems and the current precarious status of sea otter numbers in California and Alaska.

It is dusk at San Nicolas Island, California, the end of a winter's day in 1999. The sky is a monotony of low stratus clouds. We walk along the dunes above a wave-cut rocky intertidal platform. The westerly winds carry the distant eerie wails of California sea lions preparing for an evening foraging at sea. Hissing breakers spill across the rocky shore. The winds carry dampness and we are uncomfortably cool, droplets of water forming in our hair and eyebrows. With sore knees and stiff backs from a day at work, we search in vain for the reassuring vision of a sunset, finding only the penetrating wet chill. We turn for the shelter of our rusting van. Then we notice, both of us at the same time: in the water just outside the surf zone, swimming parallel to the shoreline in the failing light, are two sea otters. They are foraging along the inner edge of the kelp forests that extend far offshore. These are two of the small colony of sea otters that survive from the translocation project of the late 1980s. I feel a swell of emotion as I recall daydreams of years ago. I had visualized sea otters in this very place. Now they are here as they were in centuries past, sharing the island with the spirits of the Nicoleño people driven to extinction by the fur traders.

The sea otters pause briefly on the surface and raise their heads. They move offshore, at once lost in the gray waves and windblown spray. They seem to be at home. We retreat to the van and close the doors, flakes of corroded sheet metal clattering to the floor. The engine sputters to life and we drive east, laboring up the hill and into the fog. I steer with my left hand as, unconsciously, my right hand forms an exultant raised fist. Kristina admonishes me to use both hands on the wheel. I comply, but out of the corner of my eye I see her wide smile, her joyfully raised fist. The enveloping fog simplifies our views to shades of gray, but the image of the sea otters remains indelible, luminous, hopeful.

Like many mammals, when asleep sea otters are irresistibly anthropomorphic.

Public Involvement in Sea Otter Conservation

At present, most sea otters are found in coastal waters of the United States, Canada and Russia. In all jurisdictions with sea otter populations nearby, primary management authority rests with agencies of federal or regional governments. Requests for information about sea otters, and comments regarding policies for management, normally can be sent to these agencies.

In the United States, management authority for sea otters is held by the federal U.S. Fish and Wildlife Service (FWS). FWS offices involved with sea otter management are located in Ventura, California and Anchorage, Alaska. State agencies in the United States also have important roles in sea otter management. The California Department of Fish and Game in Sacramento, the Washington Department of Fish and Wildlife in Olympia, and the Alaska Department of Fish and Game in Anchorage can all be contacted for information about sea otter populations in their respective regions.

In Canada, sea otters fall under the management authority of a federal agency, Fisheries and Oceans Canada. The agency office with primary authority for sea otter management is located in Nanaimo, British Columbia. In Russia, primary authorities are the Academy of Sciences and the Kamchatka Fisheries Inspection Bureau, both located in Petropavlovsk-Kamchatskiy, Kamchatka and the Institute of Fisheries and Oceanography in Moscow.

Friends of the Sea Otter (FSO) is a non-governmental advocacy organization that actively promotes the protection and enhancement of sea otter populations, habitats and ecosystems in the United States. FSO is based in Monterey, California, U.S.A. Additional information about the biology and conservation of sea otters can be obtained from any of the 44 aquaria and zoological parks that have live sea otters on public display in Belgium, Canada, Japan, The Netherlands, Portugal and the United States.

Another day, another clam. Sunset at Kachemak Bay.

Sea Otters Distribution Map

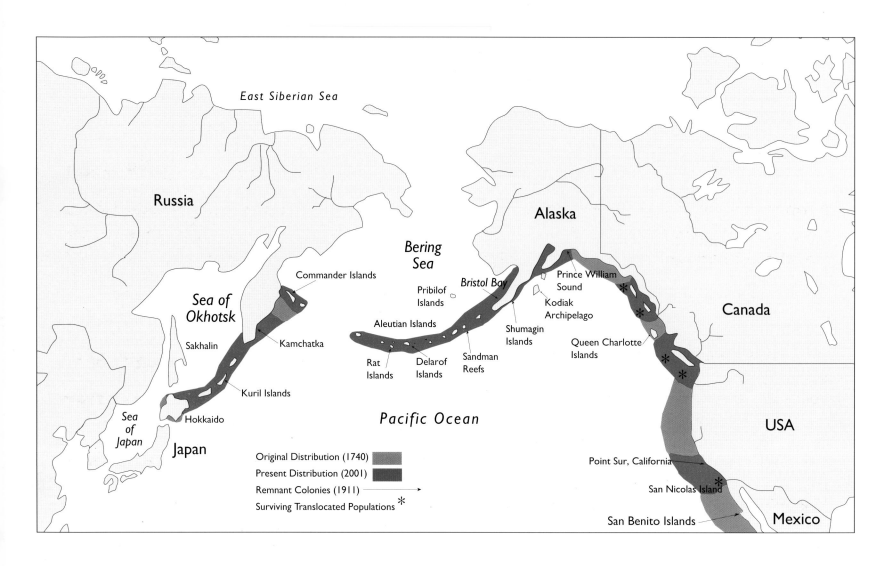

- Russia
- East Siberian Sea
- Sea of Okhotsk
- Commander Islands
- Sakhalin
- Kamchatka
- Kuril Islands
- Hokkaido
- Sea of Japan
- Japan
- Bering Sea
- Bristol Bay
- Pribilof Islands
- Aleutian Islands
- Rat Islands
- Delarof Islands
- Sandman Reefs
- Shumagin Islands
- Kodiak Archipelago
- Prince William Sound
- Alaska
- Queen Charlotte Islands
- Canada
- USA
- Point Sur, California
- San Nicolas Island
- San Benito Islands
- Mexico
- Pacific Ocean

Original Distribution (1740)
Present Distribution (2001)
Remnant Colonies (1911) ⟶
Surviving Translocated Populations *

Sea Otters Facts

Scientific Name	*Enhydra lutris*	
Adult Length	male	51 in (130 cm)
	female	47 in (120 cm)
Newborn Pup Length	24 in (60 cm)	
Adult Weight	male	66 lbs (30 kg)
	female	44 lbs (20 kg)
Newborn Pup Weight	4-5 lbs (2 kg)	
Longevity	male	10-15 years
	Female	15-20 years (one female lived for 28 years in captivity)

Breeding: Males mature sexually at about 5-6 years, but do not breed until they are a few years older and able to defend breeding territories. Females mature at 3-5 years. Gestation period is about 6 months. Pups are born singly, usually in spring, although they can be born in any month of the year. Females in good health will produce one pup per year.

Recommended Reading

There are many excellent books on sea otters ranging from detailed technical accounts and texts for a more general readership to titles relating to the biology and management of marine mammals. A representative sample is listed below.

Berta, A., & Sumich, J., (eds.) *Marine Mammals: Evolutionary Biology.* Academic Press, 1999.

Love, J. A., *Sea Otters.* London, Whittet Books, 1990.

Nickerson, R., & Bucich, R., *Sea Otters. A Natural History and Guide.* California, Chronicle Books, 1998.

Paine, S., & Foote, J., *The World of the Sea Otter.* California, Sierra Club Books, 1993.

Reynolds III, J., & Rommel, S., (eds.) *Biology of Marine Mammals.* Smithsonian Institution Press, 1999.

Riedman, M., *Sea Otters.* Monterey, Monterey Bay Aquarium, 1990.

Riedman, M., & Estes, J., *The Sea Otter: Behavior, Ecology and Natural History.* U.S. Fish and Wildlife Service, 1990.

Twiss, J., Reeves, R., & Montgomery, S., (eds.) *Conservation and Management of Marine Mammals.* Smithsonian Institution Press, 1999.

VanBlaricom, G., & Estes, J., (eds.) *The Community Ecology of Sea Otters.* Springer- Verlag, 1988.

There are also a number of useful websites that are worthy of further exploration including:

Friends of the Sea Otter http://www.seaotters.org/

American Cetacean Society http://www.acsonline.org/

Index

*Entries in **bold** indicate pictures*

Adaptations 12
Age estimation 38, 40, 41
Algae 30
Bering, Captain Vitus 49
Body form 11, 12, 42
  limbs 11, 12, 46
By-catch 62
Capture 40
Communication 46
Conservation 50, 53, 54, 57, 61, 62, 66, 69
Diseases 62
Distribution 14, 42, **70**
Diving 7, **10**, 12, 18, 21, 25, 46
Ecosystem relationships 8, 29, 30, 33, 61, 66, 69
Exploitation 14, 50, 65
Exxon Valdez 57, 58, **59**, 61
First Nations 53
Foraging 7, **10**, **16**, 17, **18**, **19**, 21, 22, **24**, 25,

26, **28**, 29, **32**, 33, 34, **35**, **41**, 45, 46, **52**, 66, **68**
Fur 11, 12, 14, 18, 45, 46, 57, 58
  harvesting 14, 33, 50, 65
Grooming **6**, 12, **15**, 17, 18, **27**, 45, **50**, 58
Habitat 8, 11, 14, 18, **20**, 21, 41, 42, 45, 54
Harbour Seals **32**
Kelp **8**, **23**, **27**, 30, **31**, **32**, 33, **36**, 42, **43**, 45, **50**, **56**, **63**
Killer Whales 61
Lactation 41, 45
Life span 40, 41
Marine Otter 11
Metabolism 14, 17, 41
Mustelidae 11
Native Americans 53, 65, 66
Oil spills 57, 58, **59**, 61
Parasites 62

Pelage see 'fur'
Poaching 53, 62
Population sizes 53, 54, 61, 62
Prey 7, 14, **16**, **18**, **19**, 21, 22, **25**, 26, **28**, 29, 30, 33, 34, **41**, 46, 61, **63**, **68**
  abalones 8, 18, 22, 25, 29, **30**, 34
  clams 7, 8, 14, 18, 22, 26, **28**, 29, 34, **68**
  crabs 8, 18, **19**, 21, 22, 26, **28**, 29, **30**, 34, **35**
  fish 14, 21
  mussels 14, 18, 21, 22, 33, 34, **41**
  octopus 8, 18
  sea urchins 8, **18**, 21, 22, 26, **28**, 29, 30, 33, 34, **63**
  snails 18, 21, **25**, 26, **30**
Pups **15**, **23**, 26, 29, 41, 42, **43**, 45, 46, **50**, **53**

Rafts **9**, **36**, **44**, 45
Reproduction 41, 42, 45
Resting **6**, **9**, 11, 21, **23**, **27**, **31**, **32**, **36**, **39**, **40**, **43**, **44**, 45, 46, **47**, **48**, **52**, **55**, **56**, **64**, **67**
Seabirds 21
Shellfishery effects 8, 34, 65
Shelter 42
Size 11, 40, 46, 71
Steller's sea cow 49, 53
Steller, G. W. 49, 50
Tagging 37, 38, 40
Teeth 14, 22, 38, 40, 41
Territoriality 41, 42, 45
Thermoregulation 12, 14, 17, 18, 46, 58, **64**
Tool use 22, 25, 26, 29
Touch 7, 21
Translocations 54, 66
Vision 21
Whaling 65

Biographical Note

Glenn VanBlaricom is an associate professor at the University of Washington, where he directs a large program in marine mammal research. He attended university during the 1960s, and it was here that he developed his lifelong interest in marine ecology. Since then, he has studied the ecology of sea otters for over 23 years, surveying populations in California, Washington, Alaska and Russia. Glenn lives in the U.S.A.